THIS BOOK BELONGS TO:

BELIEVE

A THREE MINUTE JOURNAL TO
TRANSFORM YOUR DESTINY

BRANDY MULLEN

Tellwell Talent
www.tellwell.ca

ISBN
978-0-2288-6939-9 (Hardcover)
978-0-2288-6938-2 (Paperback)

The legal stuff: While I have helped thousands of people
set and achieve their goals, I do not make any warranties
or representations with respect to the outcomes achieved
by following this journal. The strategies employed may
not work for your unique situation and you should consult
professionals whenever appropriate. In fact, some of your
action steps might be to reach out for help in an area that
you are working on. Neither the author or publisher shall
be liable for any loss of profit or any other damages.
Special thanks to Helen Hu and Teresa Liu
for their assistance with this journal.

This journal is dedicated to all the changemakers of the world!

May you listen to your heart and bravely pursue your dreams.

May you always believe in yourself and
never doubt how awesome you are!

This guided journal is built upon years of experience and practice that will help you succeed each and every day. Its carefully structured format of actionable prompts and inspirational quotes gives you a strategy for calibrating each day in as little as 3 minutes. As you use your journal, you will see your goal materialize as you implement its accompanying action steps to achieve your dreams regardless of how busy your life is or how ambitious your goals are!

This journal will help you:

Start each day with an "I've already achieved it" mindset

Focus on getting the most important things done on even the busiest days

Place yourself in a positive mindset by focusing on what you are grateful for

Direct your energy to take steps each and every day to improve your overall well-being

Encounter the power of intentionality in setting goals to achieve your biggest dreams

End each day with an optimistic mindset by highlighting daily successes and restating your goal

Because the journal will:

Inspire you with motivational quotes

Encourage you to keep reviewing your big goal and the steps to get you there

Help you to imagine yourself as already achieving your goal

INTRODUCTION

This Journal is for ordinary people dreaming of extraordinary lives. Author, Brandy Mullen once labelled herself as "ordinary" but in her heart she longed to be EXTRAordinary and to achieve personal goals beyond that. The secret she discovered was a nagging whisper in her ear getting louder and louder as time went by. The words weren't always immediately clear but the message persisted. "Go for it! Truly, fully and completely for your goals in the biggest, boldest way!" But how?

By developing a system of personalized prompts, seeking personal inspiration and applying a daily discipline to her goals, Brandy was astonished when she actually achieved one of her really BIG goals! As the success of her achievement sunk in, she set another goal, and then another…they just kept getting bigger and she just kept achieving them. As she developed a system and organized herself for a life of achievement, she realized that she could help others by providing a process for them to follow and succeed with-This Prompt Journal is the result.

Brandy created this guided journal to help people continue to reach higher and higher and achieve their biggest goals and dreams. The Prompt Journal will help people like you achieve goals that you might have thought unattainable, perhaps because of fear of failure or some other excuse or barrier. This journal is designed to give you a process and inspire you to break down those barriers, to believe in yourself and to take control of your own path to success.

HOW TO USE THIS JOURNAL

MORNING ROUTINE

At the top of each page you will see the words "I am…"

The most important thing about filling this out is to use PRESENT tense.

For example: *"I am healthy and strong"*

NOT *"I am trying to be healthy and strong"*

NOT *"I am wanting to be healthy and strong"*

NOT *"I am going to be healthy and strong"*

The process here is to harness your own belief. *Believe* in your goal and begin acting like you have already achieved it. How does a person who DOES/IS that behave? How do they go about their day? What is essential to being that person?

Next, stop and feel the truth of this thing that you want to achieve in every cell of your body. You cannot write your *"I am.."* sentence while thinking in your head that it will never happen for you. You must use the power of manifestation to believe it is true and then you must take action to make that the truth. Don't be afraid to put something big, bold, and uncomfortable down. Growth happens outside of our comfort zone and here is the chance to set a big goal and think about it every day and every night. It's your journal so dare to be brave and write something that you want but have been too afraid to go after.

This second phase of the process requires you to think about the three non-negotiable action items that you must do to be that thing that you want. What are the three things you must do if this is true/going to be true/stay true? Using the example *"I am healthy and strong"* we all know that you cannot come home after work and binge watch your favourite television show while eating an entire bag of chips. Writing *"I am healthy and strong"* not *"I am trying to be healthy and strong"* is the first step but you cannot just think it. You must use this guide to put some small action steps behind it (or large if you want to get there faster).

Here is an example of what your actions might look like:

Three non-negotiable action items:

3. *"Drink 2 liters of water"*
2. *"Go to spin class at 4 PM"*
1. *"Eat a serving of green vegetables at every meal"*

The next step in this journal is to look at other areas of your life as these will indirectly impact your ability to achieve your big goal. What other areas do you want to change? Do you want to go to bed earlier? Do you want to spend more quality time with your family? All of the things we do to look after ourselves impact our overall well-being. For example. A solid night's sleep means you will feel energized and you can then use that energy to crush your three daily non-negotiables. Everything is connected so it's important to look after all parts of self. This also means that improving one area of your life the –'I am….' - will lead to improvements in other areas as well. You just need to believe and trust the process and the process starts with one step in the right direction. It all starts with that one first step. This is where the 'Two gifts I will give to myself or others' comes in. Since we are all connected, being a go-giver will help us as well. Some days these gifts might be all for you and some days they may be things you do for others. There is no right or wrong way to fill these pages out and there is no guilt in giving yourself some gifts. And to be clear this doesn't mean buying yourself or others something… the gifts I am talking about are priceless.

Here are some examples:

2. *"Go to bed by 10 PM"*
1. *"Send a text my friend to let them know I am thinking about them"*

The last part of your morning routine is to write something that you are grateful for. By focusing on the positives in your life you will be calibrated to positivity for the day and destined to achieve those actions you set.

Here are some examples:

1. *"I am grateful for my best friend"*
1. *"I am grateful for my home"*
1. *"I am grateful for my health"*

NIGHT ROUTINE

At the end of the day come back to your three-minute journal and write out three wins for the day. What successes did you have? Did you accomplish your three non-negotiables? You could write them here! Did something else spectacular happen that you want to include? Be proud of what you accomplished and know that tomorrow is a new day.

Here are some examples:

Today's wins

3. *"Drank two liters of water"*
2. *"Attended spin class"*
1. *"Ate five servings of vegetables"*

The last thing is to re-write that magical sentence that IS your big goal/dream. 'I am…. Write this before bed and fall asleep knowing that your subconscious will do the work to help make this come true. Each and every day you will write 'I am…….' (Your big goal/dream). You will be thinking about the big goal/dream morning and night. This will reinforce it in your head and heart. It will come true if you start to think about and *believe* it to be true. Your conscious actions combined with your subconscious mind working all night for you gives you a supercharge in the direction of your goal.

Here is the example:

I am *"Healthy and strong"*

Date <u>01/01/2030</u>

> *Just one positive thought in the morning can change your whole day. Dalai Lama*

I am <u>*a terrific friend*</u>

Three non-negotiable action items

3. <u>*Text my friend to let them know I was thinking of them*</u>
2. <u>*Put phone away and give 100% of my attention when I see them tonight*</u>
1. <u>*Input a reminder in my calendar for their partner's birthday*</u>

Two gifts I will give to myself or others

2. <u>*Book a massage*</u>
1. <u>*Read 10 pages of a good book*</u>

One thing I am grateful for

1. <u>*My best friend*</u>

EVENING

Today's wins

3. <u>*Actively listened in an important meeting*</u>
2. <u>*Texted my friend and they were excited to share great news with me*</u>
1. <u>*Told my friend how much I appreciate them*</u>

I am <u>*a terrific friend*</u>

_____ / _____ / 20_____

I am_____

Three non-negotiable action items

3._____

2._____

1._____

Two gifts I will give to myself or others

2._____

1._____

One thing I am grateful for

1._____

EVENING

Today's wins

3._____

2._____

1._____

I am _____

14

_____ / _____ / 20____

> *By recording your dreams and goals on paper, you set in motion
> the process of becoming the person you most want to be. Put
> your future in good hands — your own. Mark Victor Hansen*

I am_____

Three non-negotiable action items

3._____

2._____

1._____

Two gifts I will give to myself or others

2._____

1._____

One thing I am grateful for

1._____

EVENING

Today's wins

3._____

2._____

1._____

I am _____

_____ / _____ / 20_____

> *We become what we think about most of the time,*
> *and that's the strangest secret. Earl Nightingale*

I am_____

Three non-negotiable action items

3._____
2._____
1._____

Two gifts I will give to myself or others

2._____
1._____

One thing I am grateful for

1._____

EVENING

Today's wins

3._____
2._____
1._____
I am _____

_____ / _____ / 20_____

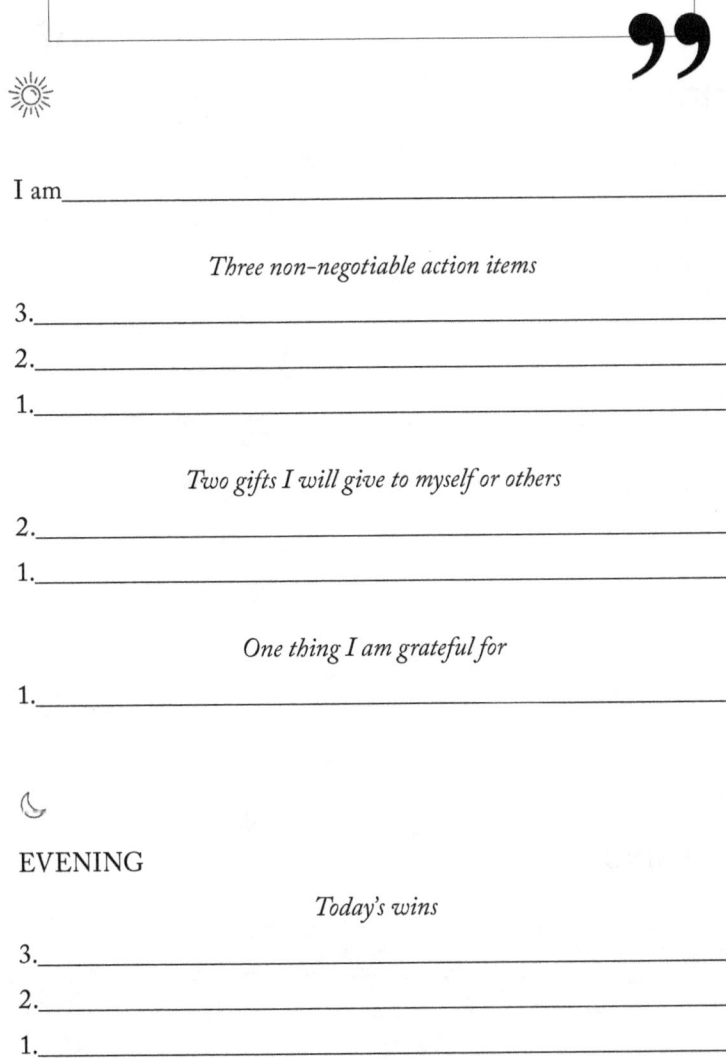

> *Don't let your fears be bigger than your dream. Amanda Hopkins*

I am_____

Three non-negotiable action items

3._____

2._____

1._____

Two gifts I will give to myself or others

2._____

1._____

One thing I am grateful for

1._____

EVENING

Today's wins

3._____

2._____

1._____

I am _____

_____ / _____ / 20_____

> *You have to learn the rules of the game. And then you have to play better than anyone else. Albert Einstein*

I am_____

Three non-negotiable action items

3._____

2._____

1._____

Two gifts I will give to myself or others

2._____

1._____

One thing I am grateful for

1._____

EVENING

Today's wins

3._____

2._____

1._____

I am _____

_____ / _____ / 20_____

I am_____

Three non-negotiable action items

3._____

2._____

1._____

Two gifts I will give to myself or others

2._____

1._____

One thing I am grateful for

1._____

EVENING

Today's wins

3._____

2._____

1._____

I am _____

_____ / _____ / 20_____

*If you really look closely, most overnight
successes took a long time. Steve Jobs*

I am_____

Three non-negotiable action items

3._____
2._____
1._____

Two gifts I will give to myself or others

2._____
1._____

One thing I am grateful for

1._____

EVENING

Today's wins

3._____
2._____
1._____
I am _____

_____ / _____ / 20____

> *Once you choose hope, anything's possible. Christopher Reeve*

I am_____

Three non-negotiable action items

3._____

2._____

1._____

Two gifts I will give to myself or others

2._____

1._____

One thing I am grateful for

1._____

EVENING

Today's wins

3._____

2._____

1._____

I am _____

_____ / _____ / 20____

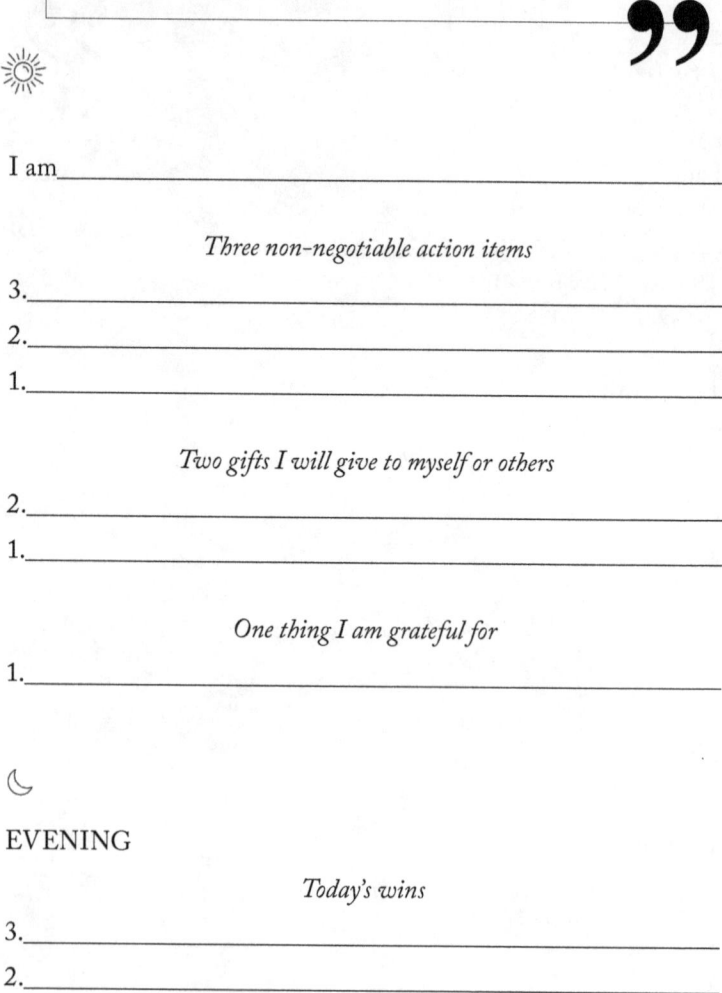

> *Once you agree upon the price you and your family must pay for success, it enables you to ignore the minor hurts, the opponent's pressure, and the temporary failures. Vince Lombardi*

I am_____

Three non-negotiable action items

3._____

2._____

1._____

Two gifts I will give to myself or others

2._____

1._____

One thing I am grateful for

1._____

EVENING

Today's wins

3._____

2._____

1._____

I am _____

_____ / _____ / 20_____

> *The first step toward success is taken when you refuse to be a captive of the environment in which you first find yourself. Mark Caine*

I am_____

Three non-negotiable action items

3._____

2._____

1._____

Two gifts I will give to myself or others

2._____

1._____

One thing I am grateful for

1._____

EVENING

Today's wins

3._____

2._____

1._____

I am _____

____ / ____ / 20____

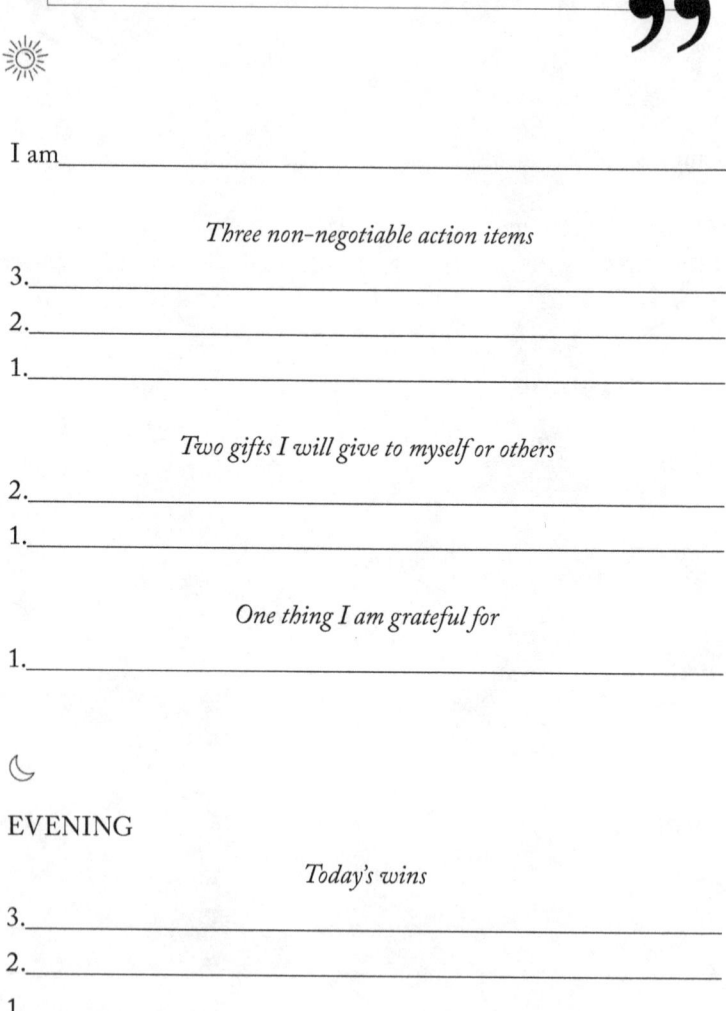

> *There are two types of people who will tell you that you cannot make a difference in this world: those who are afraid to try and those who are afraid you will succeed. Ray Goforth*

I am_____

Three non-negotiable action items

3._____
2._____
1._____

Two gifts I will give to myself or others

2._____
1._____

One thing I am grateful for

1._____

EVENING

Today's wins

3._____
2._____
1._____
I am _____

_____ / _____ / 20_____

> *Doing the best at this moment puts you in the best place for the next moment. Oprah Winfrey*

I am_____

Three non-negotiable action items

3._____

2._____

1._____

Two gifts I will give to myself or others

2._____

1._____

One thing I am grateful for

1._____

EVENING

Today's wins

3._____

2._____

1._____

I am _____

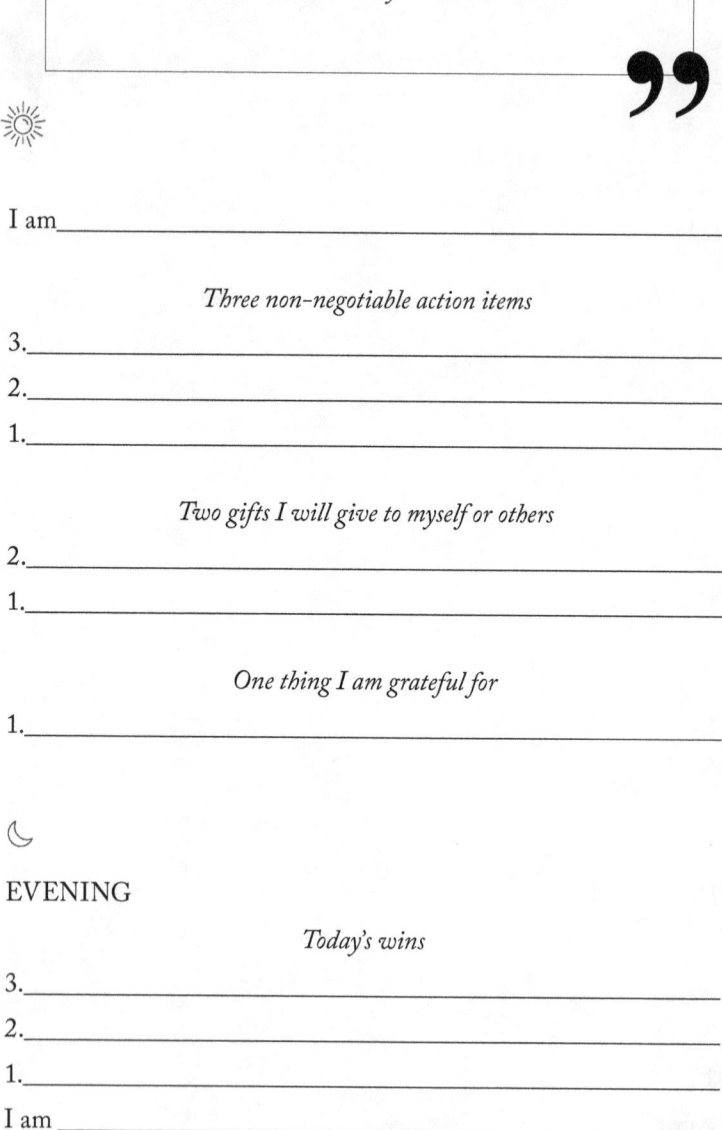

> *The road to success begins with knowing what you need to know and why. Savania China*

I am_____

Three non-negotiable action items

3._____

2._____

1._____

Two gifts I will give to myself or others

2._____

1._____

One thing I am grateful for

1._____

EVENING

Today's wins

3._____

2._____

1._____

I am _____

_____ / _____ / 20_____

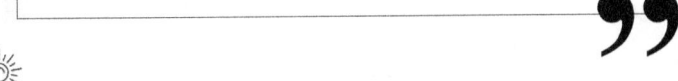

*Deciding what not to do is as important as
deciding what to do. Steve Jobs*

I am_____

Three non-negotiable action items

3._____

2._____

1._____

Two gifts I will give to myself or others

2._____

1._____

One thing I am grateful for

1._____

☾

EVENING

Today's wins

3._____

2._____

1._____

I am _____

_____ /_____ / 20___

> *The successful warrior is the average man,*
> *with laser-like focus. Bruce Lee*

☀

I am_____

Three non-negotiable action items

3._____

2._____

1._____

Two gifts I will give to myself or others

2._____

1._____

One thing I am grateful for

1._____

☾

EVENING

Today's wins

3._____

2._____

1._____

I am _____

_____ / _____ / 20_____

> *You willed yourself to where you are today, so*
> *will yourself out of it. Stephen Richards*

I am_____

Three non-negotiable action items

3._____

2._____

1._____

Two gifts I will give to myself or others

2._____

1._____

One thing I am grateful for

1._____

EVENING

Today's wins

3._____

2._____

1._____

I am _____

_____ / _____ / 20_____

> *Wealth is largely the result of habit. John Jacob Astor*

I am_____

Three non-negotiable action items

3._____

2._____

1._____

Two gifts I will give to myself or others

2._____

1._____

One thing I am grateful for

1._____

EVENING

Today's wins

3._____

2._____

1._____

I am _____

____ / ____ / 20____

> *Baby steps turn into miles over time. Deirdre Maloney*

I am_____

Three non-negotiable action items

3._____

2._____

1._____

Two gifts I will give to myself or others

2._____

1._____

One thing I am grateful for

1._____

EVENING

Today's wins

3._____

2._____

1._____

I am _____

_____ / _____ / 20_____

> *Develop success from failures. Discouragement and failure are two of the surest stepping stones to success. Dale Carnegie*

I am_____

Three non-negotiable action items

3._____

2._____

1._____

Two gifts I will give to myself or others

2._____

1._____

One thing I am grateful for

1._____

☾

EVENING

Today's wins

3._____

2._____

1._____

I am _____

_____ / _____ / 20_____

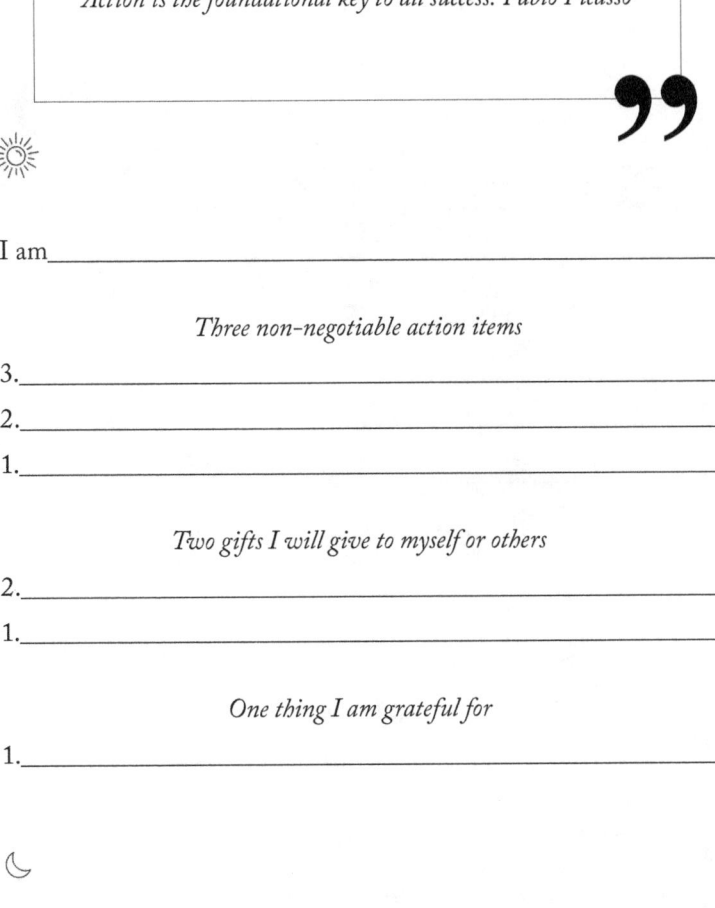

Action is the foundational key to all success. Pablo Picasso

I am_____

Three non-negotiable action items

3._____

2._____

1._____

Two gifts I will give to myself or others

2._____

1._____

One thing I am grateful for

1._____

EVENING

Today's wins

3._____

2._____

1._____

I am _____

_____ / _____ / 20_____

> *How long should I try? Until. Jim Rohn*

I am_____

Three non-negotiable action items

3._____

2._____

1._____

Two gifts I will give to myself or others

2._____

1._____

One thing I am grateful for

1._____

EVENING

Today's wins

3._____

2._____

1._____

I am _____

Our deepest fear is not that we are inadequate. Our deepest fear is that we are powerful beyond measure. It is our light, not our darkness that most frightens us. We ask ourselves, 'Who am I to be brilliant, gorgeous, talented, fabulous?' Actually, who are you not to be? You are a child of God. Your playing small does not serve the world. There is nothing enlightened about shrinking so that other people won't feel insecure around you. We are all meant to shine, as children do. We were born to make manifest the glory of God that is within us. It's not just in some of us; it's in everyone. And as we let our own light shine, we unconsciously give other people permission to do the same. As we are liberated from our own fear, our presence automatically liberates others. Marianne Williamson

Congratulations! You are three weeks into your journal. Habits are formed in as few as three weeks. Your journey is just beginning and I hope you are feeling a shift inside of you. Use this page to reflect on your last three weeks and prepare to move forward with more focus and conviction.

What are you afraid of that might be holding you back? How will you overcome this obstacle?

_____

_____

_____

_____

_____

_____

_____

_____

_____

_____

_____

_____

_____

_____ / _____ / 20_____

I am_____

Three non-negotiable action items

3._____

2._____

1._____

Two gifts I will give to myself or others

2._____

1._____

One thing I am grateful for

1._____

EVENING

Today's wins

3._____

2._____

1._____

I am _____

36

_____ / _____ / 20_____

I am_____

Three non-negotiable action items

3._____

2._____

1._____

Two gifts I will give to myself or others

2._____

1._____

One thing I am grateful for

1._____

EVENING

Today's wins

3._____

2._____

1._____

I am _____

_____ / _____ / 20_____

> *Vision without action is merely a dream. Action without vision just passes the time. Vision with action can change the world. Joel Arthur Barker*

I am_____

Three non-negotiable action items

3._____

2._____

1._____

Two gifts I will give to myself or others

2._____

1._____

One thing I am grateful for

1._____

EVENING

Today's wins

3._____

2._____

1._____

I am _____

_____ /_____ / 20_____

> _There is no chance, no destiny, no fate, that can
> circumvent or hinder or control the firm resolve
> of a determined soul. Ella Wheeler Wilcox_

I am_____

Three non-negotiable action items

3._____

2._____

1._____

Two gifts I will give to myself or others

2._____

1._____

One thing I am grateful for

1._____

EVENING

Today's wins

3._____

2._____

1._____

I am _____

_____ / _____ / 20_____

> *If you have a dream, know that I, other people, and the universe supports you. Cheryl Geonanga*

I am_____

Three non-negotiable action items

3._____

2._____

1._____

Two gifts I will give to myself or others

2._____

1._____

One thing I am grateful for

1._____

EVENING

Today's wins

3._____

2._____

1._____

I am _____

_____ /_____ / 20_____

> *Never bend your head. Always hold it high. Look*
> *the world straight in the eye. Helen Keller*

I am_____

Three non-negotiable action items

3._____

2._____

1._____

Two gifts I will give to myself or others

2._____

1._____

One thing I am grateful for

1._____

EVENING

Today's wins

3._____

2._____

1._____

I am _____

_____ / _____ / 20_____

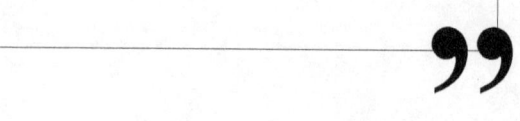

> *When you have a dream, you've got to grab it and never let go. Carol Burnett*

I am_____

Three non-negotiable action items

3._____
2._____
1._____

Two gifts I will give to myself or others

2._____
1._____

One thing I am grateful for

1._____

EVENING

Today's wins

3._____
2._____
1._____
I am _____

_____ / _____ / 20_____

> *Nothing is impossible. The word itself says "I'm possible!". Audrey Hepburn*

I am_____

Three non-negotiable action items

3._____

2._____

1._____

Two gifts I will give to myself or others

2._____

1._____

One thing I am grateful for

1._____

EVENING

Today's wins

3._____

2._____

1._____

I am _____

_____ / _____ / 20_____

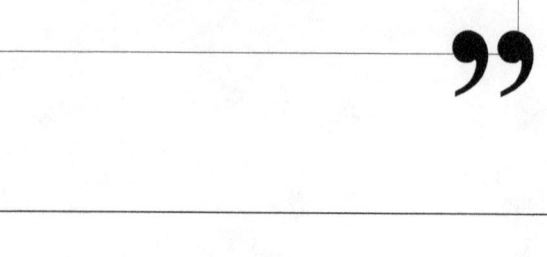

You may have to fight a battle more than once to win it. Margaret Thatcher

I am_____

Three non-negotiable action items

3._____

2._____

1._____

Two gifts I will give to myself or others

2._____

1._____

One thing I am grateful for

1._____

EVENING

Today's wins

3._____

2._____

1._____

I am _____

___ / ___ / 20___

Act as if what you do makes a difference. It does. William James

I am_____

Three non-negotiable action items

3._____

2._____

1._____

Two gifts I will give to myself or others

2._____

1._____

One thing I am grateful for

1._____

EVENING

Today's wins

3._____

2._____

1._____

I am _____

____ /____ / 20____

> *Motivation is what gets you started. Habit is what keeps you going. Jim Ryun*

I am_____

Three non-negotiable action items

3._____

2._____

1._____

Two gifts I will give to myself or others

2._____

1._____

One thing I am grateful for

1._____

EVENING

Today's wins

3._____

2._____

1._____

I am _____

_____ / _____ / 20_____

> *Sometimes you will never know the value of a moment, until it becomes a memory. Dr. Seuss*

I am_____

Three non-negotiable action items

3._____

2._____

1._____

Two gifts I will give to myself or others

2._____

1._____

One thing I am grateful for

1._____

EVENING

Today's wins

3._____

2._____

1._____

I am _____

_____ /_____ / 20___

I am_____

Three non-negotiable action items

3._____
2._____
1._____

Two gifts I will give to myself or others

2._____
1._____

One thing I am grateful for

1._____

EVENING

Today's wins

3._____
2._____
1._____
I am _____

_____ /_____ / 20_____

I am_____

Three non-negotiable action items

3._____

2._____

1._____

Two gifts I will give to myself or others

2._____

1._____

One thing I am grateful for

1._____

EVENING

Today's wins

3._____

2._____

1._____

I am _____

___ / ___ / 20___

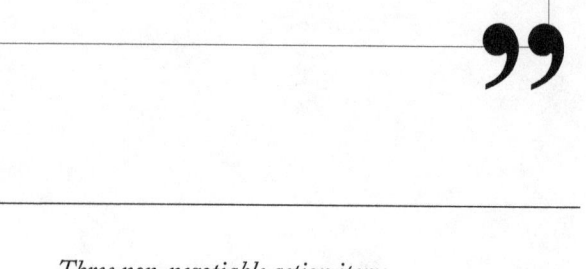

> *Some people look for a beautiful place. Others make a place beautiful. Hazrat Inayat Khan*

I am_____

Three non-negotiable action items

3._____

2._____

1._____

Two gifts I will give to myself or others

2._____

1._____

One thing I am grateful for

1._____

EVENING

Today's wins

3._____

2._____

1._____

I am _____

Happiness often sneaks in through a door you didn't know you left open. John Barrymore

I am_____

Three non-negotiable action items

3._____

2._____

1._____

Two gifts I will give to myself or others

2._____

1._____

One thing I am grateful for

1._____

EVENING

Today's wins

3._____

2._____

1._____

I am _____

Life changes very quickly, in a very positive way, if you let it. Lindsey Vonn

I am_____

Three non-negotiable action items

3._____

2._____

1._____

Two gifts I will give to myself or others

2._____

1._____

One thing I am grateful for

1._____

EVENING

Today's wins

3._____

2._____

1._____

I am _____

_____ / _____ / 20_____

> *We must be willing to let go of the life we planned, so as to have the life that is waiting for us. Joseph Campbell*

I am_____

Three non-negotiable action items

3._____

2._____

1._____

Two gifts I will give to myself or others

2._____

1._____

One thing I am grateful for

1._____

EVENING

Today's wins

3._____

2._____

1._____

I am _____

_____ / _____ / 20_____

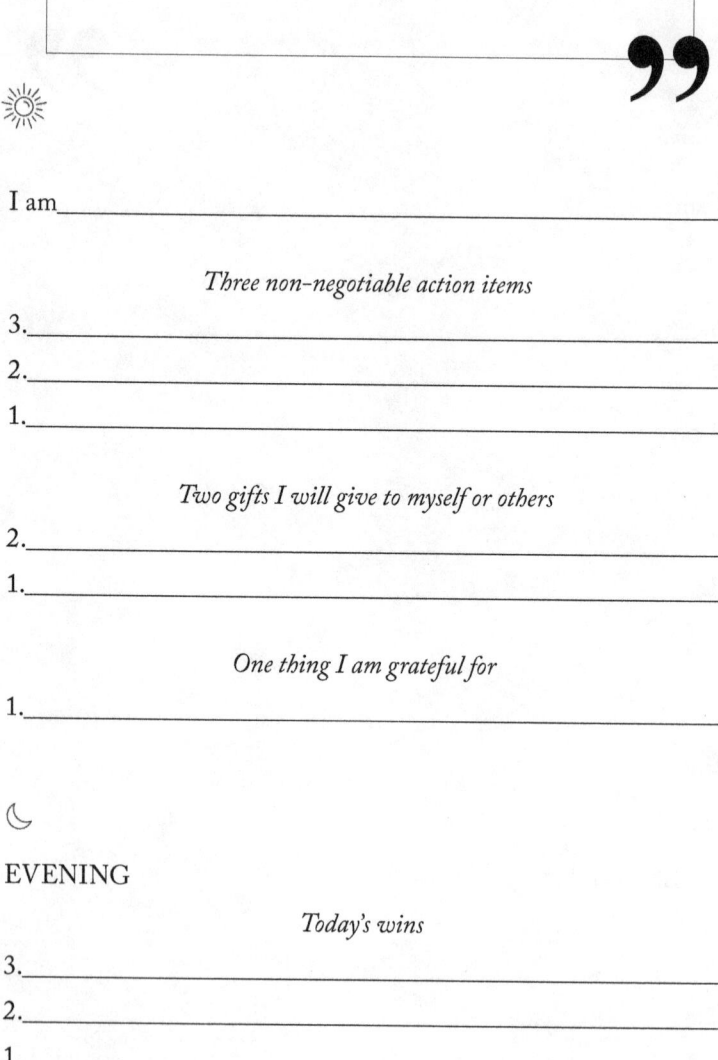

> *Failure is the condiment that gives success
> its flavor. Truman Capote*

I am_____

Three non-negotiable action items

3._____

2._____

1._____

Two gifts I will give to myself or others

2._____

1._____

One thing I am grateful for

1._____

EVENING

Today's wins

3._____

2._____

1._____

I am _____

_____ / _____ / 20_____

> *Ask yourself what success looks like for you. Then put all your energy into making it happen. Live by your own measure not someone else's. Arlene Dickinson*

I am_____

Three non-negotiable action items

3._____

2._____

1._____

Two gifts I will give to myself or others

2._____

1._____

One thing I am grateful for

1._____

EVENING

Today's wins

3._____

2._____

1._____

I am _____

_____ / _____ / 20_____

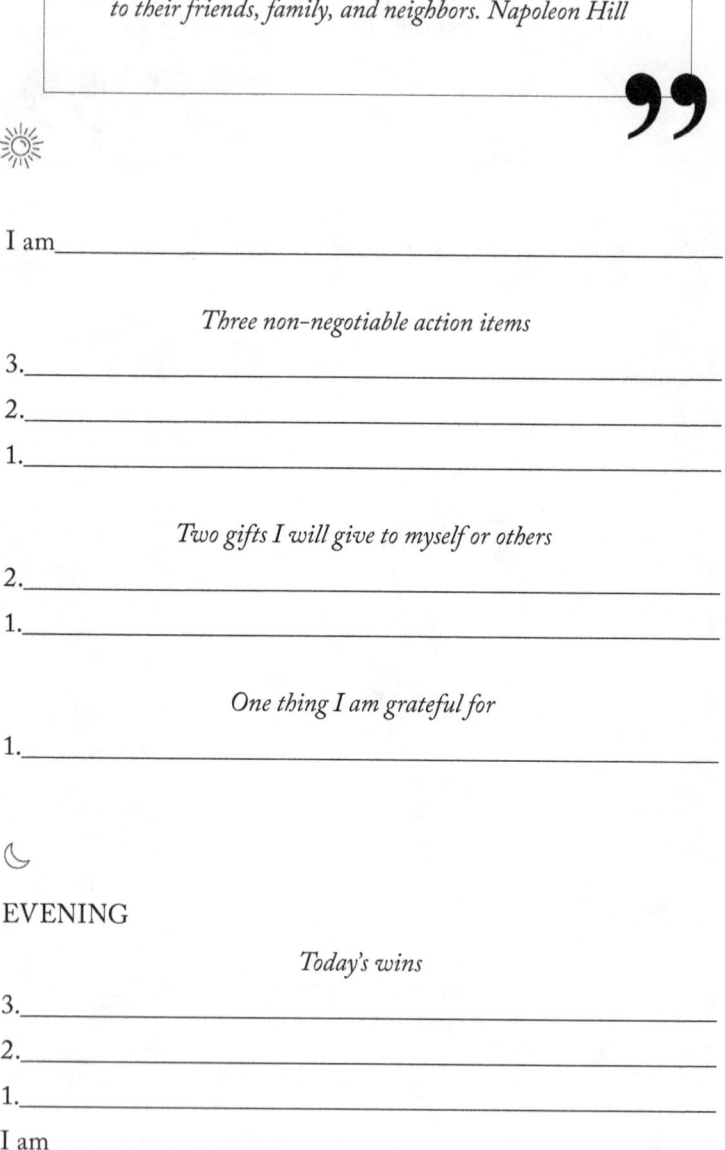

> *The number one reason people fail in life is because they listen to their friends, family, and neighbors. Napoleon Hill*

I am_____

Three non-negotiable action items

3._____

2._____

1._____

Two gifts I will give to myself or others

2._____

1._____

One thing I am grateful for

1._____

EVENING

Today's wins

3._____

2._____

1._____

I am _____

_____ / _____ / 20_____

I am _____

Three non-negotiable action items

3. _____

2. _____

1. _____

Two gifts I will give to myself or others

2. _____

1. _____

One thing I am grateful for

1. _____

EVENING

Today's wins

3. _____

2. _____

1. _____

I am _____

_____ / _____ / 20___

> *If you genuinely want something, don't wait for it--teach yourself to be impatient. Gurbaksh Chahal*

I am_____

Three non-negotiable action items

3._____

2._____

1._____

Two gifts I will give to myself or others

2._____

1._____

One thing I am grateful for

1._____

EVENING

Today's wins

3._____

2._____

1._____

I am _____

_____ /_____ / 20_____

> *I find that when you have a real interest in life and a curious life, that sleep is not the most important thing. Martha Stewart*

I am_____

Three non-negotiable action items

3._____

2._____

1._____

Two gifts I will give to myself or others

2._____

1._____

One thing I am grateful for

1._____

EVENING

Today's wins

3._____

2._____

1._____

I am _____

_____ / _____ / 20_____

I am_____

Three non-negotiable action items

3._____

2._____

1._____

Two gifts I will give to myself or others

2._____

1._____

One thing I am grateful for

1._____

EVENING

Today's wins

3._____

2._____

1._____

I am _____

_____ / _____ / 20_____

> *You miss 100% of the shots you don't take. Wayne Gretzky*

I am_____

Three non-negotiable action items

3._____
2._____
1._____

Two gifts I will give to myself or others

2._____
1._____

One thing I am grateful for

1._____

EVENING

Today's wins

3._____
2._____
1._____
I am _____

_____ / _____ / 20_____

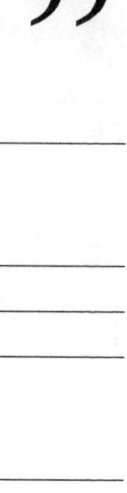

> *Comparison with myself brings improvement, comparison with others brings discontent. Betty Jamie Chung*

I am_____

Three non-negotiable action items

3._____

2._____

1._____

Two gifts I will give to myself or others

2._____

1._____

One thing I am grateful for

1._____

EVENING

Today's wins

3._____

2._____

1._____

I am _____

_____ / _____ / 20_____

> *A clear vision, backed by definite plans, gives you a tremendous feeling of confidence and personal power. Brian Tracy*

I am _____

Three non-negotiable action items

3. _____
2. _____
1. _____

Two gifts I will give to myself or others

2. _____
1. _____

One thing I am grateful for

1. _____

EVENING

Today's wins

3. _____
2. _____
1. _____
I am _____

_____ / _____ / 20_____

> *I think goals should never be easy, they should force you to work, even if they are uncomfortable at the time. Michael Phelps*

I am_____

Three non-negotiable action items

3._____

2._____

1._____

Two gifts I will give to myself or others

2._____

1._____

One thing I am grateful for

1._____

EVENING

Today's wins

3._____

2._____

1._____

I am _____

____ / ____ / 20____

I am_____

Three non-negotiable action items

3._____

2._____

1._____

Two gifts I will give to myself or others

2._____

1._____

One thing I am grateful for

1._____

EVENING

Today's wins

3._____

2._____

1._____

I am _____

_____ /_____ / 20_____

> *Today's accomplishments were yesterday's impossibilities. Robert H. Schuller*

I am_____

Three non-negotiable action items

3._____

2._____

1._____

Two gifts I will give to myself or others

2._____

1._____

One thing I am grateful for

1._____

EVENING

Today's wins

3._____

2._____

1._____

I am _____

> *The only way to do great work is to love what you do. If you haven't found it yet, keep looking. Don't settle. Steve Jobs*

I am_____

Three non-negotiable action items

3._____

2._____

1._____

Two gifts I will give to myself or others

2._____

1._____

One thing I am grateful for

1._____

EVENING

Today's wins

3._____

2._____

1._____

I am _____

_____ / _____ / 20_____

> *Do what you can with all you have, where you are. Theodore Roosevelt*

I am_____

Three non-negotiable action items

3._____

2._____

1._____

Two gifts I will give to myself or others

2._____

1._____

One thing I am grateful for

1._____

EVENING

Today's wins

3._____

2._____

1._____

I am _____

_____ / _____ / 20_____

> *Develop an 'Attitude of Gratitude'. Say thank you to everyone you meet for everything they do for you. Brian Tracy*

I am_____

Three non-negotiable action items

3._____

2._____

1._____

Two gifts I will give to myself or others

2._____

1._____

One thing I am grateful for

1._____

EVENING

Today's wins

3._____

2._____

1._____

I am _____

> *Persist – don't take no for an answer. If you're happy to sit at your desk and not take any risk, you'll be sitting at your desk for the next 20 years. David Rubenstein*

I am_____

Three non-negotiable action items

3._____

2._____

1._____

Two gifts I will give to myself or others

2._____

1._____

One thing I am grateful for

1._____

EVENING

Today's wins

3._____

2._____

1._____

I am _____

_____ /_____ / 20_____

> *If plan A fails, remember that you have*
> *25 letters left. Chris Guillebeau*

I am_____

Three non-negotiable action items

3._____

2._____

1._____

Two gifts I will give to myself or others

2._____

1._____

One thing I am grateful for

1._____

EVENING

Today's wins

3._____

2._____

1._____

I am _____

____ /____ / 20___

People often say that motivation doesn't last. Well, neither does bathing – that's why we recommend it daily. Zig Ziglar

I am____

Three non-negotiable action items

3.____

2.____

1.____

Two gifts I will give to myself or others

2.____

1.____

One thing I am grateful for

1.____

EVENING

Today's wins

3.____

2.____

1.____

I am ____

____ / ____ / 20____

> *I'm like a surfer, first you just paddle and fall off the board but as time goes by you can stand up on the bigger waves. Kim Nam-joon*

I am_____

Three non-negotiable action items

3._____

2._____

1._____

Two gifts I will give to myself or others

2._____

1._____

One thing I am grateful for

1._____

EVENING

Today's wins

3._____

2._____

1._____

I am _____

73

_____ / _____ / 20_____

> *Life is tough, and things don't always work out well, but we should be brave and go on with our lives. Min Yoongi*

I am_____

Three non-negotiable action items

3._____

2._____

1._____

Two gifts I will give to myself or others

2._____

1._____

One thing I am grateful for

1._____

EVENING

Today's wins

3._____

2._____

1._____

I am _____

74

> *You're going to have a good day. How do I know that?*
> *Because you are capable of making it a good one. Even*
> *if there's hard stuff going on, look for the good in the*
> *small moments and you'll feel it. Mel Robbins*

I am_____

Three non-negotiable action items

3._____

2._____

1._____

Two gifts I will give to myself or others

2._____

1._____

One thing I am grateful for

1._____

EVENING

Today's wins

3._____

2._____

1._____

I am _____

> *I never dreamed about success. I worked for it. Estée Lauder*

I am_____

Three non-negotiable action items

3._____

2._____

1._____

Two gifts I will give to myself or others

2._____

1._____

One thing I am grateful for

1._____

EVENING

Today's wins

3._____

2._____

1._____

I am _____

_____ / _____ / 20_____

> *Think like a queen. A queen is not afraid to fail. Failure is another stepping stone to greatness. Oprah Winfrey*

I am_____

Three non-negotiable action items

3._____

2._____

1._____

Two gifts I will give to myself or others

2._____

1._____

One thing I am grateful for

1._____

EVENING

Today's wins

3._____

2._____

1._____

I am _____

_____ /_____ / 20_____

> *You have to be unique, and different, and*
> *shine in your own way. Lady Gaga*

I am_____

Three non-negotiable action items

3._____

2._____

1._____

Two gifts I will give to myself or others

2._____

1._____

One thing I am grateful for

1._____

EVENING

Today's wins

3._____

2._____

1._____

I am _____

_____ /_____ / 20_____

> *You've got to get up every morning with determination if you're going to go to bed with satisfaction. George Lorimer*

I am_____

Three non-negotiable action items

3._____

2._____

1._____

Two gifts I will give to myself or others

2._____

1._____

One thing I am grateful for

1._____

EVENING

Today's wins

3._____

2._____

1._____

I am _____

_____ / _____ / 20___

> *Education is the most powerful weapon which you can use to change the world. Nelson Mandela*

I am_____

Three non-negotiable action items

3._____

2._____

1._____

Two gifts I will give to myself or others

2._____

1._____

One thing I am grateful for

1._____

EVENING

Today's wins

3._____

2._____

1._____

I am _____

_____ / _____ / 20_____

Take the attitude of a student, never be too big to ask questions, never know too much to learn something new. Og Mandino

I am_____

Three non-negotiable action items

3._____

2._____

1._____

Two gifts I will give to myself or others

2._____

1._____

One thing I am grateful for

1._____

EVENING

Today's wins

3._____

2._____

1._____

I am _____

> *The elevator to success is out of order. You'll have to use the stairs, one step at a time. Joe Girard*

I am_____

Three non-negotiable action items

3._____

2._____

1._____

Two gifts I will give to myself or others

2._____

1._____

One thing I am grateful for

1._____

EVENING

Today's wins

3._____

2._____

1._____

I am _____

> *Mondays are the start of the work week which offer new beginnings 52 times a year! David Dweck*

I am_____

Three non-negotiable action items

3._____

2._____

1._____

Two gifts I will give to myself or others

2._____

1._____

One thing I am grateful for

1._____

EVENING

Today's wins

3._____

2._____

1._____

I am _____

> *Who told you the lie that you could not do it?*
> *Why are you still listening to that voice? You have*
> *everything you need to live your best life. Be all in!*
>
> *Love Brandy*

I am_____

Three non-negotiable action items

3._____

2._____

1._____

Two gifts I will give to myself or others

2._____

1._____

One thing I am grateful for

1._____

EVENING

Today's wins

3._____

2._____

1._____

I am _____

_____ /_____ / 20_____

> *When your legs are tired, run with your heart. Emma Greatrix*

I am_____

Three non-negotiable action items

3._____

2._____

1._____

Two gifts I will give to myself or others

2._____

1._____

One thing I am grateful for

1._____

EVENING

Today's wins

3._____

2._____

1._____

I am _____

> *Growth is painful. Change is painful. But nothing is as painful as staying stuck somewhere you don't belong. Mandy Hale*

I am_____

Three non-negotiable action items

3._____

2._____

1._____

Two gifts I will give to myself or others

2._____

1._____

One thing I am grateful for

1._____

EVENING

Today's wins

3._____

2._____

1._____

I am _____

_____ / _____ / 20_____

Let go, let love. Kerry McInerney

I am_____

Three non-negotiable action items

3._____

2._____

1._____

Two gifts I will give to myself or others

2._____

1._____

One thing I am grateful for

1._____

EVENING

Today's wins

3._____

2._____

1._____

I am _____

_____ / _____ / 20_____

> *Every success story is a tale of constant adaptation,*
> *revision and change. Richard Branson*

I am_____

Three non-negotiable action items

3._____

2._____

1._____

Two gifts I will give to myself or others

2._____

1._____

One thing I am grateful for

1._____

EVENING

Today's wins

3._____

2._____

1._____

I am _____

_____ / _____ / 20_____

I am_____

Three non-negotiable action items

3._____

2._____

1._____

Two gifts I will give to myself or others

2._____

1._____

One thing I am grateful for

1._____

EVENING

Today's wins

3._____

2._____

1._____

I am _____

> *Do or do not. There is no try. Yoda*

I am_____

Three non-negotiable action items

3._____

2._____

1._____

Two gifts I will give to myself or others

2._____

1._____

One thing I am grateful for

1._____

EVENING

Today's wins

3._____

2._____

1._____

I am _____

_____ /_____ / 20_____

I am_____

Three non-negotiable action items

3._____

2._____

1._____

Two gifts I will give to myself or others

2._____

1._____

One thing I am grateful for

1._____

EVENING

Today's wins

3._____

2._____

1._____

I am _____

> *Someone's sitting in the shade today because someone planted a tree a long time ago. Warren Buffet*

I am_____

Three non-negotiable action items

3._____

2._____

1._____

Two gifts I will give to myself or others

2._____

1._____

One thing I am grateful for

1._____

EVENING

Today's wins

3._____

2._____

1._____

I am _____

> *The greatest discovery of my generation is that a human being can alter his life by altering his attitudes. William James*

I am_____

Three non-negotiable action items

3._____

2._____

1._____

Two gifts I will give to myself or others

2._____

1._____

One thing I am grateful for

1._____

EVENING

Today's wins

3._____

2._____

1._____

I am _____

_____ / _____ / 20_____

I am_____

Three non-negotiable action items

3._____

2._____

1._____

Two gifts I will give to myself or others

2._____

1._____

One thing I am grateful for

1._____

EVENING

Today's wins

3._____

2._____

1._____

I am _____

____ / ____ / 20____

> *Happiness is not by chance, but by choice. Jim Rohn*

I am_____

Three non-negotiable action items

3._____

2._____

1._____

Two gifts I will give to myself or others

2._____

1._____

One thing I am grateful for

1._____

EVENING

Today's wins

3._____

2._____

1._____

I am _____

_____ / _____ / 20_____

> *True freedom is impossible without a mind made free by discipline. Mortimer J. Adler*

I am_____

Three non-negotiable action items

3._____
2._____
1._____

Two gifts I will give to myself or others

2._____
1._____

One thing I am grateful for

1._____

EVENING

Today's wins

3._____
2._____
1._____
I am _____

_____ /_____ / 20_____

I am_____

Three non-negotiable action items

3._____

2._____

1._____

Two gifts I will give to myself or others

2._____

1._____

One thing I am grateful for

1._____

EVENING

Today's wins

3._____

2._____

1._____

I am _____

_____ / _____ / 20_____

> *When everything seems to be going against you, remember that the airplane takes off against the wind, not with it. Henry Ford*

I am_____

Three non-negotiable action items

3._____

2._____

1._____

Two gifts I will give to myself or others

2._____

1._____

One thing I am grateful for

1._____

EVENING

Today's wins

3._____

2._____

1._____

I am _____

_____ / _____ / 20_____

> *Don't be trapped in someone else's dream. Kim Taehyung*

I am_____

Three non-negotiable action items

3._____
2._____
1._____

Two gifts I will give to myself or others

2._____
1._____

One thing I am grateful for

1._____

EVENING

Today's wins

3._____
2._____
1._____
I am _____

____ /____ / 20____

> *Everything you've ever wanted is sitting on the other side of fear. George Addair*

I am_____

Three non-negotiable action items

3._____

2._____

1._____

Two gifts I will give to myself or others

2._____

1._____

One thing I am grateful for

1._____

EVENING

Today's wins

3._____

2._____

1._____

I am _____

_____ / _____ / 20_____

> *Just keeping swimming. Dory, Finding Nemo*

I am_____

Three non-negotiable action items

3._____

2._____

1._____

Two gifts I will give to myself or others

2._____

1._____

One thing I am grateful for

1._____

EVENING

Today's wins

3._____

2._____

1._____

I am _____

_____ / _____ / 20_____

> *What you do makes a difference and you have to decide what kind of difference you want to make. Jane Goodall*

I am_____

Three non-negotiable action items

3._____

2._____

1._____

Two gifts I will give to myself or others

2._____

1._____

One thing I am grateful for

1._____

EVENING

Today's wins

3._____

2._____

1._____

I am _____

> *You can't be that kid standing at the top of the waterslide, overthinking it. You have to go down the chute. Tina Fey*

I am_____

Three non-negotiable action items

3._____

2._____

1._____

Two gifts I will give to myself or others

2._____

1._____

One thing I am grateful for

1._____

EVENING

Today's wins

3._____

2._____

1._____

I am _____

____ /____ / 20____

> *We must zoom out to see the full picture. Wellness Warrior*

I am_____

Three non-negotiable action items

3._____
2._____
1._____

Two gifts I will give to myself or others

2._____
1._____

One thing I am grateful for

1._____

EVENING

Today's wins

3._____
2._____
1._____
I am _____

_____ / _____ / 20_____

> *I didn't learn to be quiet when I had an opinion. The reason they knew who I was is because I told them. Ursula Burns*

I am_____

Three non-negotiable action items

3._____

2._____

1._____

Two gifts I will give to myself or others

2._____

1._____

One thing I am grateful for

1._____

EVENING

Today's wins

3._____

2._____

1._____

I am _____

_____ / _____ / 20_____

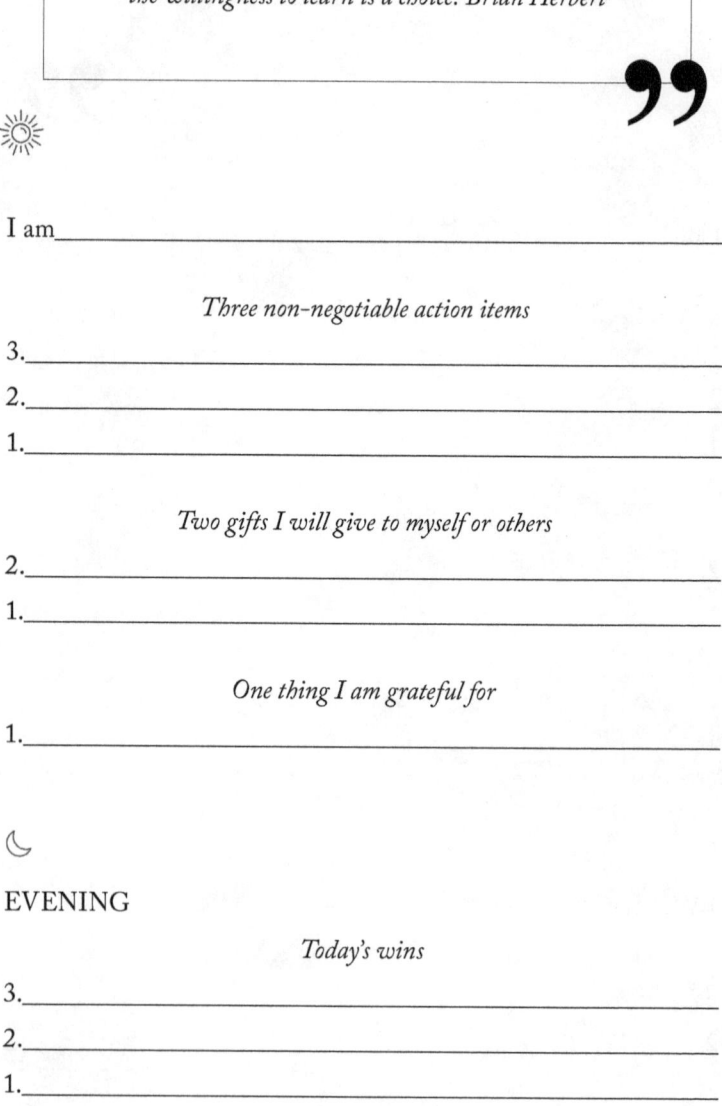

> *The capacity to learn is a gift; the ability to learn is a skill; the willingness to learn is a choice. Brian Herbert*

I am_____

Three non-negotiable action items

3._____

2._____

1._____

Two gifts I will give to myself or others

2._____

1._____

One thing I am grateful for

1._____

EVENING

Today's wins

3._____

2._____

1._____

I am _____

_____ / _____ / 20_____

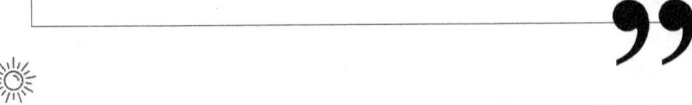

> *Success is no accident. It is hard work, perseverance, learning, studying, sacrifice and most of all, love of what you are doing or learning to do. Edson Arantes do Nascimento*

I am_____

Three non-negotiable action items

3._____

2._____

1._____

Two gifts I will give to myself or others

2._____

1._____

One thing I am grateful for

1._____

EVENING

Today's wins

3._____

2._____

1._____

I am _____

CELEBRATION TIME

A huge congratulations to you! You are now three months into writing your journal. This is the perfect opportunity to reflect on where you started, where you are going, and how you will get there. These mile markers give us an extra push to move faster, refocus, and seek help where needed. What do you need to START doing to move you closer to your goal? What do you need to STOP doing because it isn't helpful? What do you need to CONTINUE doing in order to *believe* anything (your goal) is possible?

START:

_____

_____

_____

_____

_____

STOP:

_____

_____

_____

_____

CONTINUE:

_____

_____

_____

_____

That's OK, tomorrow is a new day. Georgie's nanny ♥

_____ /_____ / 20___

I am_____

Three non-negotiable action items

3._____

2._____

1._____

Two gifts I will give to myself or others

2._____

1._____

One thing I am grateful for

1._____

EVENING

Today's wins

3._____

2._____

1._____

I am _____

> *One penny may seem to you a very insignificant thing, but it is the small seed from which fortunes spring. Orison Swett Marden*

I am_____

Three non-negotiable action items

3._____

2._____

1._____

Two gifts I will give to myself or others

2._____

1._____

One thing I am grateful for

1._____

☾

EVENING

Today's wins

3._____

2._____

1._____

I am _____

_____ / _____ / 20_____

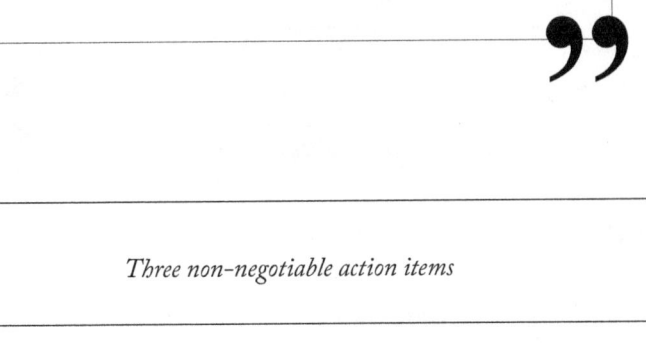

> *It's about being alive and feisty and not sitting down and shutting up, even if people would like you to.* PINK

I am_____

Three non-negotiable action items

3._____

2._____

1._____

Two gifts I will give to myself or others

2._____

1._____

One thing I am grateful for

1._____

EVENING

Today's wins

3._____

2._____

1._____

I am _____

_____ / _____ / 20_____

> *Being the change you want to see in the world doesn't require unusual courage or scary action. It only requires that you stop telling yourself that things will change while at the same time recycling the same old attitudes, beliefs, fears, blindness, conditioning, and apathy.* Deepak Chopra

I am_____

Three non-negotiable action items

3._____

2._____

1._____

Two gifts I will give to myself or others

2._____

1._____

One thing I am grateful for

1._____

EVENING

Today's wins

3._____

2._____

1._____

I am _____

_____ /_____ / 20_____

> *If you don't value your time, neither will others.*
> *Stop giving away your time and talents. Value what*
> *you know & start charging for it. Kim Garst*

I am_____

Three non-negotiable action items

3._____

2._____

1._____

Two gifts I will give to myself or others

2._____

1._____

One thing I am grateful for

1._____

EVENING

Today's wins

3._____

2._____

1._____

I am _____

_____ / _____ / 20_____

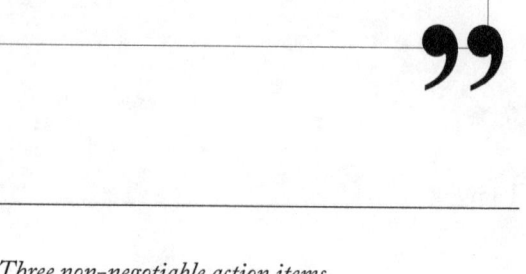

> *The only place where success comes before work*
> *is in the dictionary. Vince Lambardi*

I am_____

Three non-negotiable action items

3._____

2._____

1._____

Two gifts I will give to myself or others

2._____

1._____

One thing I am grateful for

1._____

EVENING

Today's wins

3._____

2._____

1._____

I am _____

_____ / _____ / 20_____

> *You know what you need to do to achieve this goal.*
> *Now is the time for action! Brandy Mullen*

I am_____

Three non-negotiable action items

3._____

2._____

1._____

Two gifts I will give to myself or others

2._____

1._____

One thing I am grateful for

1._____

EVENING

Today's wins

3._____

2._____

1._____

I am _____

_____ / _____ / 20_____

> *Success is not final; failure is not fatal: It is the courage to continue that counts. Winston S. Churchill*

I am_____

Three non-negotiable action items

3._____

2._____

1._____

Two gifts I will give to myself or others

2._____

1._____

One thing I am grateful for

1._____

EVENING

Today's wins

3._____

2._____

1._____

I am _____

> *There are three ways to ultimate success: The first way is to be kind. The second way is to be kind. The third way is to be kind. Mister Fred Rogers*

I am_____

Three non-negotiable action items

3._____

2._____

1._____

Two gifts I will give to myself or others

2._____

1._____

One thing I am grateful for

1._____

EVENING

Today's wins

3._____

2._____

1._____

I am _____

_____ / _____ / 20_____

I am_____

Three non-negotiable action items

3._____

2._____

1._____

Two gifts I will give to myself or others

2._____

1._____

One thing I am grateful for

1._____

EVENING

Today's wins

3._____

2._____

1._____

I am _____

_____ / _____ / 20_____

I am_____

Three non-negotiable action items

3._____

2._____

1._____

Two gifts I will give to myself or others

2._____

1._____

One thing I am grateful for

1._____

EVENING

Today's wins

3._____

2._____

1._____

I am _____

> *Keep being awesome. Brandy Mullen*

I am_____

Three non-negotiable action items

3._____
2._____
1._____

Two gifts I will give to myself or others

2._____
1._____

One thing I am grateful for

1._____

EVENING

Today's wins

3._____
2._____
1._____
I am _____

_____ / _____ / 20_____

> *The reason we struggle with insecurity is because we compare our behind-the-scenes with everyone else's highlight reel. Steve Furtick*

I am_____

Three non-negotiable action items

3._____

2._____

1._____

Two gifts I will give to myself or others

2._____

1._____

One thing I am grateful for

1._____

EVENING

Today's wins

3._____

2._____

1._____

I am _____

> *I can't tell you how many times I've been given a no. Only to find that a better, brighter, bigger yes was right around the corner. Arlan Hamilton*

I am_____

Three non-negotiable action items

3._____

2._____

1._____

Two gifts I will give to myself or others

2._____

1._____

One thing I am grateful for

1._____

EVENING

Today's wins

3._____

2._____

1._____

I am _____

_____ / _____ / 20_____

> *For the great doesn't happen through impulse alone, and is a succession of little things that are brought together. Vincent van Gogh*

I am_____

Three non-negotiable action items

3._____

2._____

1._____

Two gifts I will give to myself or others

2._____

1._____

One thing I am grateful for

1._____

EVENING

Today's wins

3._____

2._____

1._____

I am _____

_____ / _____ / 20_____

> *Do not stop thinking of life as an adventure. You have no security unless you can live bravely, excitingly, imaginatively; unless you can choose a challenge instead of competence. Eleanor Roosevelt*

I am_____

Three non-negotiable action items

3._____

2._____

1._____

Two gifts I will give to myself or others

2._____

1._____

One thing I am grateful for

1._____

EVENING

Today's wins

3._____

2._____

1._____

I am _____

_____ / _____ / 20_____

> *You are allowed to be cautious but you don't always have to be afraid. Chanel Miller*

I am_____

Three non-negotiable action items

3._____

2._____

1._____

Two gifts I will give to myself or others

2._____

1._____

One thing I am grateful for

1._____

EVENING

Today's wins

3._____

2._____

1._____

I am _____

____ / ____ / 20____

> *Success isn't always about 'Greatness', it's about consistency. Consistent hard work gains success. Greatness will come. Dwayne Johnson*

I am_____

Three non-negotiable action items

3._____

2._____

1._____

Two gifts I will give to myself or others

2._____

1._____

One thing I am grateful for

1._____

EVENING

Today's wins

3._____

2._____

1._____

I am _____

_____ / _____ / 20_____

> "You can't have a million dollar dream on a minimum wage work ethic. Stephen Hogan

I am_____

Three non-negotiable action items

3._____

2._____

1._____

Two gifts I will give to myself or others

2._____

1._____

One thing I am grateful for

1._____

EVENING

Today's wins

3._____

2._____

1._____

I am _____

_____ / _____ / 20_____

> *Don't wait for your feelings to change to take the action. Take the action and your feelings will change. Barbara Baron*

I am_____

Three non-negotiable action items

3._____

2._____

1._____

Two gifts I will give to myself or others

2._____

1._____

One thing I am grateful for

1._____

EVENING

Today's wins

3._____

2._____

1._____

I am _____

____ / ____ / 20____

> *You measure the size of the accomplishment by the obstacles you had to overcome to reach your goals. Booker T. Washington*

I am_____

Three non-negotiable action items

3._____

2._____

1._____

Two gifts I will give to myself or others

2._____

1._____

One thing I am grateful for

1._____

EVENING

Today's wins

3._____

2._____

1._____

I am _____

> *If my mind can conceive it and my heart can believe it then I can achieve it. Muhammad Ali*

I am_____

Three non-negotiable action items

3._____

2._____

1._____

Two gifts I will give to myself or others

2._____

1._____

One thing I am grateful for

1._____

EVENING

Today's wins

3._____

2._____

1._____

I am _____

___/___/20___

The work you do while you procrastinate is probably the work you should be doing for the rest of your life. Jessica Hische

I am____

Three non-negotiable action items

3.____

2.____

1.____

Two gifts I will give to myself or others

2.____

1.____

One thing I am grateful for

1.____

EVENING

Today's wins

3.____

2.____

1.____

I am ____

____ / ____ / 20____

> *There are only two options regarding commitment.*
> *You're either in or you're out. There is no such*
> *thing as life in-between. Pat Riley*

I am_____

Three non-negotiable action items

3._____

2._____

1._____

Two gifts I will give to myself or others

2._____

1._____

One thing I am grateful for

1._____

EVENING

Today's wins

3._____

2._____

1._____

I am _____

> *Where there is a will, there is a way. If there is a chance in a million that you can do something, anything, to keep what you want from ending, do it. Pry the door open or, if need be, wedge your foot in that door and keep it open. Pauline Kael*

I am_____

Three non-negotiable action items

3._____

2._____

1._____

Two gifts I will give to myself or others

2._____

1._____

One thing I am grateful for

1._____

EVENING

Today's wins

3._____

2._____

1._____

I am _____

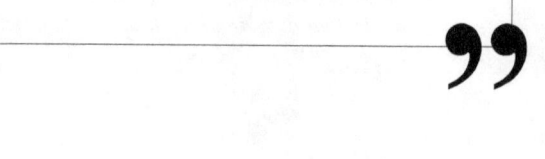

> *Just when the caterpillar thought the world was ending, it turned into a butterfly. Chuang Tzu*

I am_____

Three non-negotiable action items

3._____

2._____

1._____

Two gifts I will give to myself or others

2._____

1._____

One thing I am grateful for

1._____

EVENING

Today's wins

3._____

2._____

1._____

I am _____

_____ / _____ / 20_____

> *The difference between the impossible and the possible lies in a person's determination. Tommy Lasorda*

I am_____

Three non-negotiable action items

3._____

2._____

1._____

Two gifts I will give to myself or others

2._____

1._____

One thing I am grateful for

1._____

EVENING

Today's wins

3._____

2._____

1._____

I am _____

> *Live with intention. Walk to the edge. Listen hard. Practice wellness. Play with abandon. Laugh. Choose with no regret. Appreciate your friends. Continue to learn. Do what you love. Live as if this is all there is. Mary Anne Roadacher-Hershey*

I am_____

Three non-negotiable action items

3._____

2._____

1._____

Two gifts I will give to myself or others

2._____

1._____

One thing I am grateful for

1._____

EVENING

Today's wins

3._____

2._____

1._____

I am _____

_____ / _____ / 20_____

> *Don't downgrade your dream just to fit your reality. Upgrade your conviction to match your destiny. Stuart Scott*

I am_____

Three non-negotiable action items

3._____

2._____

1._____

Two gifts I will give to myself or others

2._____

1._____

One thing I am grateful for

1._____

EVENING

Today's wins

3._____

2._____

1._____

I am _____

> *Motivation is a fire from within. If someone else tries to light that fire under you, chances are it will burn very briefly. Stephen R Covey*

I am_____

Three non-negotiable action items

3._____

2._____

1._____

Two gifts I will give to myself or others

2._____

1._____

One thing I am grateful for

1._____

EVENING

Today's wins

3._____

2._____

1._____

I am _____

_____ / _____ / 20_____

> *When you've got something to prove, there's nothing greater than a challenge. Terry Bradshaw*

I am_____

Three non-negotiable action items

3._____

2._____

1._____

Two gifts I will give to myself or others

2._____

1._____

One thing I am grateful for

1._____

EVENING

Today's wins

3._____

2._____

1._____

I am _____

_____ / _____ / 20_____

I am_____

Three non-negotiable action items

3._____

2._____

1._____

Two gifts I will give to myself or others

2._____

1._____

One thing I am grateful for

1._____

EVENING

Today's wins

3._____

2._____

1._____

I am _____

_____ / _____ / 20_____

> *You must not let anyone define your limits because of where you come from. Your only limit is your soul. Walt Disney*

I am _____

Three non-negotiable action items

3. _____
2. _____
1. _____

Two gifts I will give to myself or others

2. _____
1. _____

One thing I am grateful for

1. _____

EVENING

Today's wins

3. _____
2. _____
1. _____
I am _____

_____ / _____ / 20_____

> *We don't have to do all of it alone. We were never meant to. Brené Brown*

I am_____

Three non-negotiable action items

3._____
2._____
1._____

Two gifts I will give to myself or others

2._____
1._____

One thing I am grateful for

1._____

EVENING

Today's wins

3._____
2._____
1._____
I am _____

_____ / _____ / 20_____

> *I wake up every morning believing today is going to be better than yesterday. Will Smith*

I am_____

Three non-negotiable action items

3._____

2._____

1._____

Two gifts I will give to myself or others

2._____

1._____

One thing I am grateful for

1._____

EVENING

Today's wins

3._____

2._____

1._____

I am _____

> *When I win and when I lose, I take ownership of it,*
> *because I really am in charge of what I do. Nicki Minaj*

I am_____

Three non-negotiable action items

3._____
2._____
1._____

Two gifts I will give to myself or others

2._____
1._____

One thing I am grateful for

1._____

EVENING

Today's wins

3._____
2._____
1._____
I am _____

_____ / _____ / 20_____

I am_____

Three non-negotiable action items

3._____
2._____
1._____

Two gifts I will give to myself or others

2._____
1._____

One thing I am grateful for

1._____

EVENING

Today's wins

3._____
2._____
1._____
I am _____

> *The two most powerful warriors are*
> *patience and time. Leo Tolstoy*

I am_____

Three non-negotiable action items

3._____

2._____

1._____

Two gifts I will give to myself or others

2._____

1._____

One thing I am grateful for

1._____

EVENING

Today's wins

3._____

2._____

1._____

I am _____

____ / ____ / 20____

> *No matter what people tell you, words and ideas*
> *can change the world. Robin Williams*

I am_____

Three non-negotiable action items

3._____

2._____

1._____

Two gifts I will give to myself or others

2._____

1._____

One thing I am grateful for

1._____

EVENING

Today's wins

3._____

2._____

1._____

I am _____

_____ / _____ / 20_____

> *Being AUTHENTIC requires self-awareness, self-discipline, self-love, self-care & COURAGE. Tim Tsai*

I am_____

Three non-negotiable action items

3._____

2._____

1._____

Two gifts I will give to myself or others

2._____

1._____

One thing I am grateful for

1._____

EVENING

Today's wins

3._____

2._____

1._____

I am _____

> *Fill the unforgiving minute with 60 seconds worth of distance run. Rudyard Kipling*

I am_____

Three non-negotiable action items

3._____

2._____

1._____

Two gifts I will give to myself or others

2._____

1._____

One thing I am grateful for

1._____

EVENING

Today's wins

3._____

2._____

1._____

I am _____

> *Use what you have, to get what you need, so you can have what you want. Vince Lee*

I am_____

Three non-negotiable action items

3._____

2._____

1._____

Two gifts I will give to myself or others

2._____

1._____

One thing I am grateful for

1._____

EVENING

Today's wins

3._____

2._____

1._____

I am _____

_____ / _____ / 20_____

> *Your future is created by what you do today,*
> *not tomorrow. Robert T. Kiyosaki*

I am_____

Three non-negotiable action items

3._____

2._____

1._____

Two gifts I will give to myself or others

2._____

1._____

One thing I am grateful for

1._____

EVENING

Today's wins

3._____

2._____

1._____

I am _____

_____ /_____ / 20_____

> *Action may not always bring happiness; but there is no happiness without action. Benjamin Disraeli*

I am_____

Three non-negotiable action items

3._____

2._____

1._____

Two gifts I will give to myself or others

2._____

1._____

One thing I am grateful for

1._____

EVENING

Today's wins

3._____

2._____

1._____

I am _____

> *Always make a total effort, even when the odds are against you. Arnold Palmer*

I am_____

Three non-negotiable action items

3._____

2._____

1._____

Two gifts I will give to myself or others

2._____

1._____

One thing I am grateful for

1._____

EVENING

Today's wins

3._____

2._____

1._____

I am _____

> *To accomplish great things, we must not only act, but also dream, not only plan, but also believe. Anatole France*

I am_____

Three non-negotiable action items

3._____

2._____

1._____

Two gifts I will give to myself or others

2._____

1._____

One thing I am grateful for

1._____

EVENING

Today's wins

3._____

2._____

1._____

I am _____

_____ / _____ / 20_____

> *Do not wait; the time will never be 'just right.' Start where you stand, and work with whatever tools you may have at your command, and better tools will be found as you go along. George Herbert*

I am_____

Three non-negotiable action items

3._____

2._____

1._____

Two gifts I will give to myself or others

2._____

1._____

One thing I am grateful for

1._____

EVENING

Today's wins

3._____

2._____

1._____

I am _____

> *I've missed more than 9,000 shots in my career. I've lost almost 300 games. Twenty-six times I've been trusted to take the game winning shot and missed. I've failed over and over and over again in my life. And that is why I succeed. Michael Jordan*

I am_____

Three non-negotiable action items

3._____

2._____

1._____

Two gifts I will give to myself or others

2._____

1._____

One thing I am grateful for

1._____

EVENING

Today's wins

3._____

2._____

1._____

I am _____

_____ / _____ / 20_____

How you do anything is how you do everything. Cheri Huber

I am_____

Three non-negotiable action items

3._____

2._____

1._____

Two gifts I will give to myself or others

2._____

1._____

One thing I am grateful for

1._____

EVENING

Today's wins

3._____

2._____

1._____

I am _____

> *The truest, most beautiful life never promises to be an easy one. We need to let go of the lie that it's supposed to be. Glennon Doyle*

I am_____

Three non-negotiable action items

3._____

2._____

1._____

Two gifts I will give to myself or others

2._____

1._____

One thing I am grateful for

1._____

☾

EVENING

Today's wins

3._____

2._____

1._____

I am _____

_ /_ / 20_

> *Desire is the key to motivation, but it's determination and commitment to an unrelenting pursuit of your goal — a commitment to excellence — that will enable you to attain the success you seek. Mario Andretti*

I am_____

Three non-negotiable action items

3._____

2._____

1._____

Two gifts I will give to myself or others

2._____

1._____

One thing I am grateful for

1._____

EVENING

Today's wins

3._____

2._____

1._____

I am _____

> *If an egg is broken by an outside force, life ends. If broken by an inside force, life begins. Great things always begin from the inside. Jim Kwik*

I am_____

Three non-negotiable action items

3._____

2._____

1._____

Two gifts I will give to myself or others

2._____

1._____

One thing I am grateful for

1._____

EVENING

Today's wins

3._____

2._____

1._____

I am _____

_____ / _____ / 20_____

> *The individual who says it is not possible should move out of the way of those doing it. Tricia Cunningham*

I am_____

Three non-negotiable action items

3._____

2._____

1._____

Two gifts I will give to myself or others

2._____

1._____

One thing I am grateful for

1._____

🌙

EVENING

Today's wins

3._____

2._____

1._____

I am _____

> *Believe in yourself! Have faith in your abilities! Without a humble but reasonable confidence in your own powers you cannot be successful or happy. Norman Vincent Peale*

I am_____

Three non-negotiable action items

3._____

2._____

1._____

Two gifts I will give to myself or others

2._____

1._____

One thing I am grateful for

1._____

EVENING

Today's wins

3._____

2._____

1._____

I am _____

____ / ____ / 20____

> *The tragedy in life doesn't lie in not reaching your goal. The tragedy lies in having no goal to reach. Benjamin Mays*

I am_____

Three non-negotiable action items

3._____

2._____

1._____

Two gifts I will give to myself or others

2._____

1._____

One thing I am grateful for

1._____

EVENING

Today's wins

3._____

2._____

1._____

I am _____

_____ /_____ / 20_____

> *All our dreams can come true if we have the*
> *courage to pursue them. Walt Disney*

I am_____

Three non-negotiable action items

3._____
2._____
1._____

Two gifts I will give to myself or others

2._____
1._____

One thing I am grateful for

1._____

EVENING

Today's wins

3._____
2._____
1._____
I am _____

> *When you are grateful, fear disappears and abundance appears. Tony Robbins*

I am_____

Three non-negotiable action items

3._____

2._____

1._____

Two gifts I will give to myself or others

2._____

1._____

One thing I am grateful for

1._____

EVENING

Today's wins

3._____

2._____

1._____

I am _____

_____ / _____ / 20_____

> *A positive mindset brings positive things. Phillip Reiter*

I am_____

Three non-negotiable action items

3._____

2._____

1._____

Two gifts I will give to myself or others

2._____

1._____

One thing I am grateful for

1._____

EVENING

Today's wins

3._____

2._____

1._____

I am _____

_____ / _____ / 20_____

> *We make a living by what we get, but we make a life by what we give. Winston Churchill*

I am_____

Three non-negotiable action items

3._____

2._____

1._____

Two gifts I will give to myself or others

2._____

1._____

One thing I am grateful for

1._____

EVENING

Today's wins

3._____

2._____

1._____

I am _____

> *What you lack in talent can be made up with desire, hustle and giving 110% all the time. Don Zimmer*

I am_____

Three non-negotiable action items

3._____

2._____

1._____

Two gifts I will give to myself or others

2._____

1._____

One thing I am grateful for

1._____

EVENING

Today's wins

3._____

2._____

1._____

I am _____

_____ / _____ / 20_____

> *Inspiration comes from within yourself. One has to be positive.*
> *When you're positive, good things happen. Deep Roy*

I am_____

Three non-negotiable action items

3._____

2._____

1._____

Two gifts I will give to myself or others

2._____

1._____

One thing I am grateful for

1._____

EVENING

Today's wins

3._____

2._____

1._____

I am _____

____ / ____ / 20____

> *Just don't give up trying to do what you really want to do. Where there is love and inspiration, I don't think you can go wrong. Ella Fitzgerald*

I am_____

Three non-negotiable action items

3._____
2._____
1._____

Two gifts I will give to myself or others

2._____
1._____

One thing I am grateful for

1._____

EVENING

Today's wins

3._____
2._____
1._____
I am _____

_____ /_____ / 20_____

> *It is our attitude at the beginning of a difficult task which, more than anything else, will affect its successful outcome. William James*

I am_____

Three non-negotiable action items

3._____

2._____

1._____

Two gifts I will give to myself or others

2._____

1._____

One thing I am grateful for

1._____

EVENING

Today's wins

3._____

2._____

1._____

I am _____

_____ / _____ / 20_____

> *You must do the things you think you cannot do. Eleanor Roosevelt*

☀

I am_____

Three non-negotiable action items

3._____

2._____

1._____

Two gifts I will give to myself or others

2._____

1._____

One thing I am grateful for

1._____

☾

EVENING

Today's wins

3._____

2._____

1._____

I am _____

_____ / _____ / 20_____

> *The world is waiting for your greatness, your gifts are inside of you waiting to be shared, don't let self-doubt or fear steal those gifts. Brandy Mullen*

I am_____

Three non-negotiable action items

3._____

2._____

1._____

Two gifts I will give to myself or others

2._____

1._____

One thing I am grateful for

1._____

EVENING

Today's wins

3._____

2._____

1._____

I am _____

> *Take up one idea. Make that one idea your life--think of it, dream of it, live on that idea. Let the brain, muscles, nerves, every part of your body, be full of that idea, and just leave every other idea alone. This is the way to success. Swami Vivekananda*

I am_____

Three non-negotiable action items

3._____

2._____

1._____

Two gifts I will give to myself or others

2._____

1._____

One thing I am grateful for

1._____

EVENING

Today's wins

3._____

2._____

1._____

I am _____

___ / ___ / 20___

> *To love is to give, to risk is to live, to fail is to succeed, to let go is to be free. Madison Kittel*

I am_____

Three non-negotiable action items

3._____

2._____

1._____

Two gifts I will give to myself or others

2._____

1._____

One thing I am grateful for

1._____

🌙

EVENING

Today's wins

3._____

2._____

1._____

I am _____

_____ / _____ / 20_____

> *We may encounter many defeats but we must
> not be defeated. Maya Angelou*

I am_____

Three non-negotiable action items

3._____

2._____

1._____

Two gifts I will give to myself or others

2._____

1._____

One thing I am grateful for

1._____

EVENING

Today's wins

3._____

2._____

1._____

I am _____

> *We generate fears while we sit. We overcome them by action. Dr. Henry Link*

I am_____

Three non-negotiable action items

3._____

2._____

1._____

Two gifts I will give to myself or others

2._____

1._____

One thing I am grateful for

1._____

🌙

EVENING

Today's wins

3._____

2._____

1._____

I am _____

Can you *believe* it? You are three weeks away from completing this journal. Keep going on this beautiful journey. Please consider reordering your next Believe journal from our website

www.believejournal.ca

Congratulations on making it this far into your journey of achieving your big goal! Can you believe how far you have come?! Look back at the beginning of this journal to see where you started. Sometimes when you are busy working on those day-to-day action steps you forget just how much you have accomplished. Be proud of all that you have done to get where you are today and keep going on this adventure called life!

____ / ____ / 20____

> *I am so proud of YOU*

I am_____

Three non-negotiable action items

3._____

2._____

1._____

Two gifts I will give to myself or others

2._____

1._____

One thing I am grateful for

1._____

EVENING

Today's wins

3._____

2._____

1._____

I am _____

> *Whenever you see a successful person you only see the public glories, never the private sacrifices to reach them. Vaibhav Shah*

I am_____

Three non-negotiable action items

3._____

2._____

1._____

Two gifts I will give to myself or others

2._____

1._____

One thing I am grateful for

1._____

EVENING

Today's wins

3._____

2._____

1._____

I am _____

> *For every reason it's not possible, there are hundreds of people who have faced the same circumstances and succeeded. Jack Canfield*

I am_____

Three non-negotiable action items

3._____

2._____

1._____

Two gifts I will give to myself or others

2._____

1._____

One thing I am grateful for

1._____

🌙

EVENING

Today's wins

3._____

2._____

1._____

I am _____

____ /____ / 20___

Whether you think you can, or you think you can't–you're right. Henry Ford

I am____

Three non-negotiable action items

3.____

2.____

1.____

Two gifts I will give to myself or others

2.____

1.____

One thing I am grateful for

1.____

EVENING

Today's wins

3.____

2.____

1.____

I am ____

> *Your doubts create mountains, Your actions move them. Mel Robbins*

I am_____

Three non-negotiable action items

3._____

2._____

1._____

Two gifts I will give to myself or others

2._____

1._____

One thing I am grateful for

1._____

EVENING

Today's wins

3._____

2._____

1._____

I am _____

_____ / _____ / 20___

> *The pessimist sees difficulty in every opportunity. The optimist sees opportunity in every difficulty. Winston Churchill*

I am_____

Three non-negotiable action items

3._____

2._____

1._____

Two gifts I will give to myself or others

2._____

1._____

One thing I am grateful for

1._____

EVENING

Today's wins

3._____

2._____

1._____

I am _____

_____ / _____ / 20_____

I am_____

Three non-negotiable action items

3._____

2._____

1._____

Two gifts I will give to myself or others

2._____

1._____

One thing I am grateful for

1._____

EVENING

Today's wins

3._____

2._____

1._____

I am _____

> *The swiftest way to triple your success is to double your investment in personal development. Robin Sharma*

I am_____

Three non-negotiable action items

3._____
2._____
1._____

Two gifts I will give to myself or others

2._____
1._____

One thing I am grateful for

1._____

EVENING

Today's wins

3._____
2._____
1._____
I am _____

_____ / _____ / 20_____

> *Every champion was once a contender who refused to give up. Rocky Balboa*

I am_____

Three non-negotiable action items

3._____

2._____

1._____

Two gifts I will give to myself or others

2._____

1._____

One thing I am grateful for

1._____

EVENING

Today's wins

3._____

2._____

1._____

I am _____

*I've got a theory that if you give 100% all the time,
somehow things will work out in the end. Larry Bird*

I am_____

Three non-negotiable action items

3._____

2._____

1._____

Two gifts I will give to myself or others

2._____

1._____

One thing I am grateful for

1._____

EVENING

Today's wins

3._____

2._____

1._____

I am _____

___ / ___ / 20___

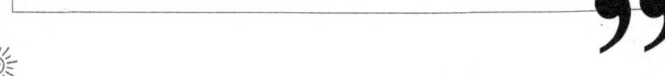

> *It's impossible to live without failing at something, unless you live so cautiously that you might as well not have lived at all- in which case you fail by default. J.K. Rowling*

I am_____

Three non-negotiable action items

3._____

2._____

1._____

Two gifts I will give to myself or others

2._____

1._____

One thing I am grateful for

1._____

🌙

EVENING

Today's wins

3._____

2._____

1._____

I am _____

> *Don't go through life, grow through life. Eric Butterworth*

I am_____

Three non-negotiable action items

3._____

2._____

1._____

Two gifts I will give to myself or others

2._____

1._____

One thing I am grateful for

1._____

EVENING

Today's wins

3._____

2._____

1._____

I am _____

_____ /_____ / 20_____

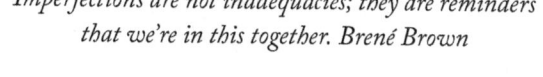

*Imperfections are not inadequacies; they are reminders
that we're in this together. Brené Brown*

I am_____

Three non-negotiable action items

3._____

2._____

1._____

Two gifts I will give to myself or others

2._____

1._____

One thing I am grateful for

1._____

☾

EVENING

Today's wins

3._____

2._____

1._____

I am _____

_____ / _____ / 20_____

> *The only way of discovering the limits of the possible is to venture a little way past them into the impossible. Arthur C. Clarke*

I am_____

Three non-negotiable action items

3._____

2._____

1._____

Two gifts I will give to myself or others

2._____

1._____

One thing I am grateful for

1._____

EVENING

Today's wins

3._____

2._____

1._____

I am _____

_____ / _____ / 20_____

> *One of the differences between some successful and unsuccessful people is that one group is full of doers, while the other is full of wishers. Edmond Mbiaka*

I am_____

Three non-negotiable action items

3._____

2._____

1._____

Two gifts I will give to myself or others

2._____

1._____

One thing I am grateful for

1._____

EVENING

Today's wins

3._____

2._____

1._____

I am _____

_____ / _____ / 20___

> *Without continual growth and progress, such words as improvement, achievement, and success have no meaning. Benjamin Franklin*

I am_____

Three non-negotiable action items

3._____

2._____

1._____

Two gifts I will give to myself or others

2._____

1._____

One thing I am grateful for

1._____

EVENING

Today's wins

3._____

2._____

1._____

I am _____

_____ / _____ / 20_____

> *Just breathe and believe. Jodi Livon*

I am_____

Three non-negotiable action items

3._____

2._____

1._____

Two gifts I will give to myself or others

2._____

1._____

One thing I am grateful for

1._____

EVENING

Today's wins

3._____

2._____

1._____

I am _____

_____ /_____ / 20___

☀

I am_____

Three non-negotiable action items

3._____

2._____

1._____

Two gifts I will give to myself or others

2._____

1._____

One thing I am grateful for

1._____

☾

EVENING

Today's wins

3._____

2._____

1._____

I am _____

_____ / _____ / 20_____

> *Keep going. That's all you have to do ever. You really don't have to be amazing or fierce or beautiful or successful or good. Just keep going, please. Slowly is fine. Crawling is fine. No feeling is final. Except hope. Glennon Doyle*

I am_____

Three non-negotiable action items

3._____
2._____
1._____

Two gifts I will give to myself or others

2._____
1._____

One thing I am grateful for

1._____

EVENING

Today's wins

3._____
2._____
1._____
I am _____

_____ / _____ / 20_____

> *Believe in yourself. You are braver than you think,*
> *more talented than you know, and capable of*
> *more than you imagine. Roy T. Bennett*

I am_____

Three non-negotiable action items

3._____
2._____
1._____

Two gifts I will give to myself or others

2._____
1._____

One thing I am grateful for

1._____

EVENING

Today's wins

3._____
2._____
1._____
I am _____

_____ / _____ / 20_____

> *I'd rather regret the things I've done than regret
> the things I haven't done. Lucille Ball*

I am_____

Three non-negotiable action items

3._____

2._____

1._____

Two gifts I will give to myself or others

2._____

1._____

One thing I am grateful for

1._____

EVENING

Today's wins

3._____

2._____

1._____

I am _____

ACKNOWLEDGEMENTS

A heartfelt appreciation to you. Whether someone gifted this to you, or you bought it yourself, I am proud of you for focusing on your dreams. Too many of us spend too much time on autopilot. You deserve a full and rich life, you deserve abundance, and you deserve to be all that you ever imagined you could be.

Thank you for being uniquely YOU! Thank you for taking a chance. Thank you for trying something new. Thank you for not settling or shrinking your goals to fit your current situation. Thank you for making the world a better place by fully showing up and living your best life!

BIOGRAPHY

For over fifteen years, Brandy Mullen has been teaching people all over the world and from all walks of life how to achieve their goals. As a professional learning strategist, she has developed unique strategies and tactics that have helped thousands to focus, plan and act on the things that create personal success. These strategies include critical skills such as how to goal set, manage time, organize, read, write and study effectively. Above all, Brandy provides the tools that help people *believe* they can achieve their goals and turn their dreams into reality. As a successful entrepreneur and educator she brings the worlds of planning and execution together for successful achievement.

CPSIA information can be obtained
at www.ICGtesting.com
Printed in the USA
LVHW101152210223
740031LV00001B/101

9 780228 869399